THE DEFINITIVE GUIDE TO MASTERING BITCOIN & CRYPTOCURRENCIES

TRADE & INVEST CRYPTOCURRENCIES WITH CONFIDENCE

WAYNE WALKER

TABLE OF CONTENTS

Introduction

Congratulations on your personal copy of *The Definitive Guide to Mastering Bitcoin & Cryptocurrencies.* We begin our journey away from the world of government issued currencies to cryptocurrencies. The first five chapters will give you a solid introduction to the cryptocurrency universe, where you will be introduced to a wide range of topics from blockchain to mining. You will also acquire a broad and deep understanding of the mechanics behind one of the most popular cryptocurrencies. The emphasis shifts in the remaining chapters to practical applications for trading. You will be introduced to trading strategies along with the know-how on how to apply them. You will also learn to exploit practical technical analysis indicators that can increase your money-making ability. This includes the often overlooked area of trader psychology. These sections are a bonus to traders of all types. Thanks for choosing this book!

Note: Throughout the book the words digital, crypto and cryptocurrency will be used interchangeably.

Chapter 1: What is Bitcoin (BTC)?

Bitcoin is a decentralized digital currency (a digital asset). It's not a stock, a tangible asset, or an actual coin. No government owns it. You can transfer money quickly without governments or banks for a low fee. In its base form it is a big spread sheet, a secure public ledger. Before money, there were ledgers. This is how primitive societies kept track of who had and did what. Cryptocurrencies, as many say, are a natural evolution in the history of money, from bartering, to coins, to paper money, to digital.

Secure ?

How secure is it? What if someone or some group hacked the ledger? Even if 40-49% were hacked, the majority would have the correct info (the ledger is decentralized). As long as the majority of the ledgers agree, the transaction is valid. If some entity tried for a 51% (majority) attack, you should be aware that an attack of this magnitude would require funds in the area of 500 million dollars to carry out. In addition, an attack of this size would be noticed relatively quickly by the network.

Keys and Wallets

There is a secret private key and a public verification key. The private key is what gives you access to your account. The public key is used to send or receive money, unless you have the private key you are unable to move a coin. Your "wallet" contains your private key. A Bitcoin wallet is loosely the equivalent of a physical wallet. Your wallet also shows your transactions on the ledger.

Why Bitcoin (BTC)?

Moving money or settling transactions is expensive and cumbersome. There are the obstacles of currency spreads, taxes, banking fees, and transaction days. The average foreign wire transfer fee in the United States and elsewhere is expensive. From corporate treasurers to the migrants who want to send money home to relatives, all dislike the traditional transfer fees. With Bitcoin, money can be moved for a nominal fee. This has the ability to assist billions of persons who do not have access to banking services. This is also an option to those suffering under high Inflation and currency controls in countries (at the time of writing) like Venezuela, Zimbabwe, etc.

A Basic BTC Transaction

A) Sarah wants to send Phillip 20 Bitcoins
B) Sarah has 100 Bitcoins
C) Sarah prepares a "transaction" and sends it out onto the blockchain*
D) Enough "miners" confirm that the transactions in a block* are legitimate. Phillip decides how much validation he needs. Even if a few miners are not trustworthy, the bulk of them will be and we can trust that the transaction between them is valid.
E) Bitcoins are transferred

* Blockchain: A **public** record/ledger of Bitcoin transactions
* Block: Is a record in the blockchain that contains and confirms waiting transactions

BTC Believers

The list of people with a positive view of Bitcoin includes influential names such as Bill Gates, Richard Branson, and Peter Thiel. Other backers include venture capitalists (VC's) and Bitcoin startups with over 1 Billion US dollars invested so far. Another example is BitAngels, a Bitcoin focused investor group looking to scale startups.

Some of the major companies considering or already accepting Bitcoin payments are, Subway, Wordpress, Virgin Galactic, Reddit, Wikipedia, Shopify, OKCupid, Amazon, Paypal, and Ebay. This is only a snapshot. For small business owners, this creates a new pool of potential clients.

Bitcoin History (Quick Version)

Satoshi Nakamoto: What We Know

- Author of the white paper and original Bitcoin software
- Not a real name. The real identity is unknown, could be; she, he, or they/corporate entity
- Rarely heard from since 2010
- Owns many Bitcoins from early mining

History

2009-2011: Enthusiast in forums spreading ideas but no real traction. Genesis block established January 3, 2009

2012-13: First bit of attention from investors, risk takers, entrepreneurs

2013-2014: Big VC's began investing

2015: Wall Street and institutions began seriously investing

2016-present: Retail traders, "man on the street" enter in noticeable numbers

Bitcoin's Many "deaths"

Bitcoin has "died" 150+ times. Below are just a few of the wildly inaccurate predications of Bitcoin's demise.

- August 11, 2013 "Why Bitcoin Is Doomed To Fail" – moneygeek | $93.43
- November 16, 2013 "Bitcoin Is A Joke" – Business Insider | $433.57
- May 4, 2017 "The Beginning of the End for Bitcoin" – Daily Reckoning | $1541.90
- July 12, 2017 "Bitcoin acceptance is virtually zero and shrinking" – Yahoo Finance | $2410.55

Bitcoin Crashes and Troubles

- 2011-2013: Saw major price bubbles and crashes
- February 2014: Mt. Gox, a Bitcoin exchange, filed in Tokyo for bankruptcy. The company lost almost 750,000 of its customers' Bitcoins, plus 100,000 of its own, worth around $473 million at the time of filing. Mt. Gox believes that the bitcoins were stolen, and blamed hackers.

Suggestion: Do due diligence, *but* be careful about using the results of one private company as judgment on an entire industry.

Bitcoin Anonymous?

Bitcoin is **not** a 100% anonymous, the addresses are public keys. The addresses however are not connected to your real world identity. To create a new identity you simply create a new public key, this is called pseudonymity.
Blockchain based currencies are publicly and permanently traceable, every coin has a history and you can see all previous

transactions. True anonymity requires pseudonymity and unlinkability. In other words, different transactions of the same user with the network should not be linkable to each other. Without anonymity, privacy is much worse than traditional banking!

Unlinkability

With unlinkability it is hard to link the different addresses of the same user. It is also difficult to connect different transactions of the same user and to link the sender of a payment to its recipient. Why is this needed? Many Bitcoin services require a real identity. For example, online wallets and exchanges, some regulated, keep records which removes your anonymity with these services.

Chapter 2: The Mechanics of Bitcoin

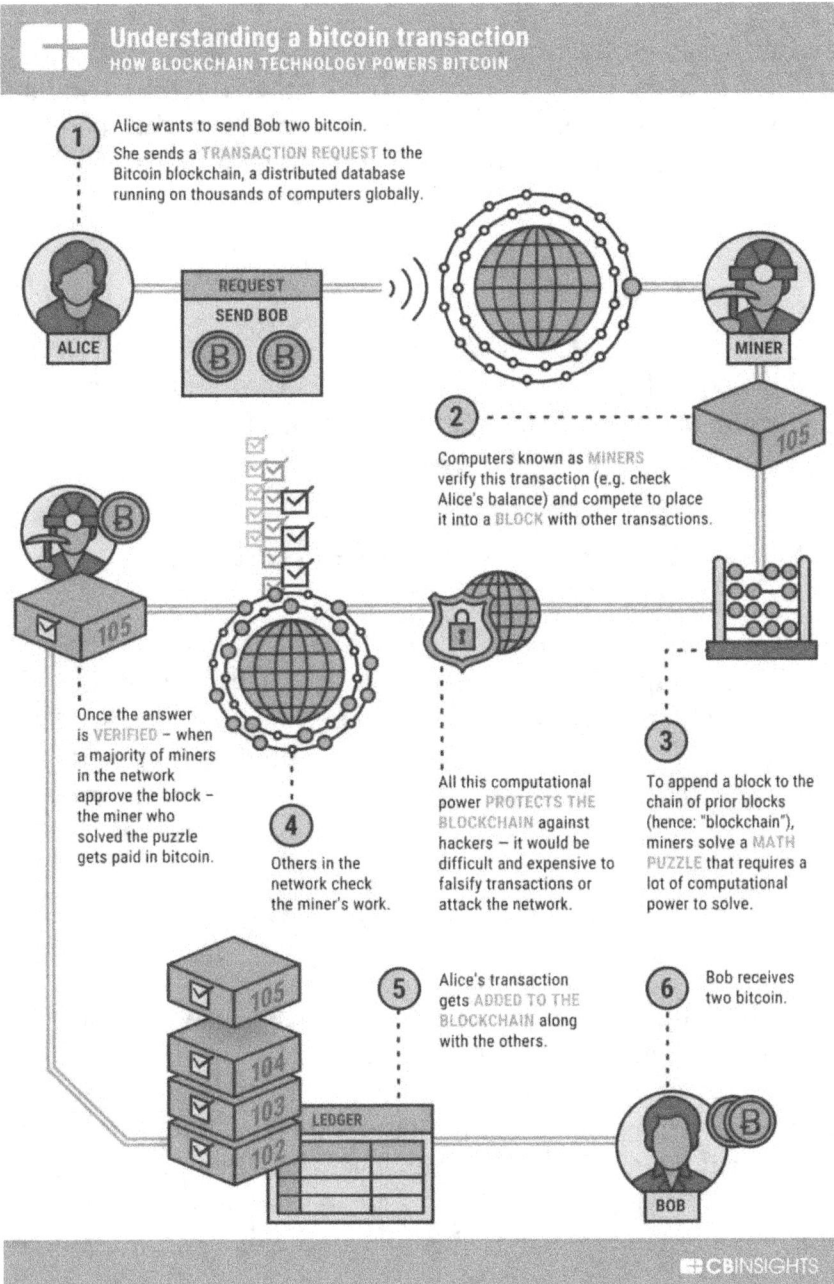

Understanding a bitcoin transaction
HOW BLOCKCHAIN TECHNOLOGY POWERS BITCOIN

1 Alice wants to send Bob two bitcoin.

She sends a TRANSACTION REQUEST to the Bitcoin blockchain, a distributed database running on thousands of computers globally.

REQUEST
SEND BOB

ALICE

MINER

2 Computers known as MINERS verify this transaction (e.g. check Alice's balance) and compete to place it into a BLOCK with other transactions.

105

Once the answer is VERIFIED – when a majority of miners in the network approve the block – the miner who solved the puzzle gets paid in bitcoin.

105

4 Others in the network check the miner's work.

All this computational power PROTECTS THE BLOCKCHAIN against hackers – it would be difficult and expensive to falsify transactions or attack the network.

3 To append a block to the chain of prior blocks (hence: "blockchain"), miners solve a MATH PUZZLE that requires a lot of computational power to solve.

5 Alice's transaction gets ADDED TO THE BLOCKCHAIN along with the others.

6 Bob receives two bitcoin.

105
104
103
LEDGER
102

BOB

CBINSIGHTS

7

Bitcoin Core Software: The Rulebook of Bitcoin

The Bitcoin Core Software is open source, (MIT license). Open source is software with "source code" that anyone can inspect, modify, and enhance. This "source code" is the code that programmers can manipulate to change how a piece of software or program works.

Storage of Bitcoins

We will take a look at some of the ways that you can store and keep track of coins. There are hot (online) and cold (offline) storage options available for your coins.

Software Wallets – Benefits/Risks

A software wallet is a relatively simple method. You store your key in a file on your computer or phone. It is convenient, but if the device is lost, the key is lost which means your coins are lost. In other words, it is only as secure as your device. If your device is hacked and the key is leaked then most likely your coins will be stolen.

Online Wallets – Benefits/Risks

An online wallet is similar to a local software wallet but it's in cyberspace. A site stores the keys and you log in to access the wallet. It is convenient with nothing to install and it works on multiple devices. The security concerns are well-known. It is vulnerable if the site is compromised (internally or externally). Be aware that your private key(s) are stored on another server, with thousands of other keys which could entice hackers to launch an attack.

Paper & Hardware Wallets – Benefits/Risks

A paper wallet is printing your public and private keys on paper and locking up the paper. More secure than the online counterparts, however, a paper wallet can be torn, water-damaged, stolen, or destroyed in many other ways. It is important to make multiple copies and keep them secure.

Hardware wallets are USB shaped stand-alone devices that generate keys while making a   transaction. They do need to be plugged into your computer while making the transaction. The wallets are secured from potential computer malware because they generate private keys offline, on the devices themselves. They are convenient and relatively easy to use. They provide backup options, plus they can also be secured with a password to combat theft. Overall, hardware wallets are the more secure option.

Bitcoin Exchanges

Exchanges accept deposits of Bitcoins (BTC) and fiat currencies ($, €) with a promise to pay back on demand. They allow customers to make/receive Bitcoin payments, buy/sell Bitcoins for fiat currencies, and match Bitcoin buyers with sellers.

An example of a common transaction: My account at the exchange has $5000 + 3 BTC, I use the exchange to buy 2 BTC for $1000 each, end result: my account has $3000 + 5 BTC.

Regulations: Banks vs Exchanges

With traditional banks, the government typically:

- Imposes minimum reserve requirements
- Insures deposits

With exchanges, the regulations varies substantially from country to country. However, there are several that have earned the trust of the market.

Bitcoin Geek Details

- 100 M *Satoshis* per Bitcoin
- 21M total Bitcoins
- 1 MB(megabyte*) each block, which is about 7 transactions per second, keep in mind
- VISA can process 2,000-10,000 transactions per second
- *One megabyte is one million bytes of information

Chapter 3: Bitcoin Mining

The mining process is one of the keys to preventing fraud. Miners confirm the authenticity of the Bitcoin transactions contained in a block. They do this by taking each transaction's corresponding data and using it to complete a math problem. The solution is known as a "hash", a shorter unique string of digits that has the important transaction information within the block. The miners are rewarded in return with 12.5 coins for their efforts.

Miners

Bitcoin miners join the network, listen for transactions and validate all proposed transactions. They also listen for new blocks, maintain the blockchain and when a new block is proposed, they validate it. The total supply of Bitcoins is 21 million. Unless the rules change they run out in 2040.

Mining Requirements and Hardware

Mining needs massive amounts of electricity! This is used to perform the computations 24/7, 365 days a year. Next on the list, are the high cooling requirements, this is needed to protect the machines. The ideal temperature in mining centers is between 15-25°C (59-77°F).

Hardware

On a high-end PC it would take years to find a block, therefore you need something a lot faster. Bitcoin ASICs are Bitcoin mining hardware. They outperform other platforms for Bitcoin mining in speed and efficiency. Bitcoin ASIC chips generally can *only be used for Bitcoin mining*. With ASIC chips the time needed to find a block drops significantly. They are designed to be run constantly for life and they also require significant expertise.

Mining Pools

Solo mining is very difficult. Even with the latest mining hardware, unless you have access to incredibly cheap power, you could eventually end up spending all your money on electricity bills. Therefore, small miners pool their risk and the pool's participants attempt to mine blocks. They distribute the revenues (transaction fees, along with newly created Bitcoins) to members based on how much work they have performed, minus the pool manager's fee.

The first pools appeared in 2010 and by 2015 around 90% of mining was pool-based. However, today major mining centers dominate. Professional mining centers are possible when the following conditions are in place: cheap power, good network and a cool climate. Since they operate 24/7, 365 days a year, a larger mining center (20,000+ machines), uses 40 megawatts of electricity per hour, the average amount used by 12,000 homes during the same period. They can pay up to $40,000 a day for electricity, even with the discounts that they normally receive.

Mining Block Rewards

Currently, block rewards are the majority of miners revenue. It is expected that in the future transaction fees will dominate. The Bitcoin block mining reward halves every 210,000 blocks, and the current coin reward will decrease from 12.5 to 6.25 coins.

Chapter 4: Bitcoin Community and Politics

A Bitcoin Improvement Proposal (BIP) is a formal proposal for changes to Bitcoin. It includes technical specifications and the basis for them. Anyone in the world can propose a BIP. It is up to the Bitcoin community of users, miners, developers, and investors to vote and decide whether or not to implement proposals.

In the Bitcoin community, the Core Developers rule changes are followed by default. What if users don't like a rule change? They can exit or exercise their right to "fork" the rules or software. A fork is a change to the software of a digital currency that creates two separate versions of the blockchain with a shared history.

Soft & Hard Fork Possibilities

Soft forks can lead to new signature schemes and extra per block metadata. Hard forks can lead to changes to size limits and changes to the mining rate.

A hard fork is a permanent divergence in the blockchain, it occurs when non-upgraded nodes can't validate blocks created by upgraded nodes that follow newer consensus rules. A node is a computer that connects to the Bitcoin network.

After a hard fork, if the fork was meant to start an altcoin (alternative currency), the altcoin goes its separate way, they coexist. If the fork reflected a fight over the future of Bitcoin then the sides fight for market share to be seen as the "real Bitcoin" one wins, the other might fade away. In the case of Bitcoin Cash they co-exist.

Hard fork example: Bitcoin Cash is similar to Bitcoin, except that it increases the size of a block from 1MB to 8MB. Why was this needed? If a transaction doesn't make it onto a block that is sent into the network for validation, it has to wait, and this slows down the process. Increasing the size of a block results in faster transactions.

Who Has The Power In Bitcoin?

There are many opinions on who has the "real" power in Bitcoin. For now we will work with the principle that it depends on who wins the fight if they fail to agree. Below is a brief description of the different players.

Bitcoin Power Brokers

Investors - Determine whether Bitcoin has any market value
Bitcoin Core Developers - They write the rulebook
Miners - Write the history and validate transactions
Merchants and their customers - They generate the primary demand and long-term price for Bitcoins

In addition to the above players, there is the Bitcoin Foundation (founded 2012). The foundation pays Core Developers and speak to governments as the representative of Bitcoin.

Chapter 5: Regulations

Governments are very much aware of Bitcoin. The attention is attracted because you have untraceable digital cash that circumvents capital controls and countries can't stop Bitcoin value from flowing in or out.

So can no one stop Bitcoin? Hmm...Bitcoin could be banned through regulation of the communication operators (communication is subject to regulation). Bitcoin is a type of internet traffic that can be stopped as any other. If a government were to decide suddenly
that no one in their country can access Bitcoin, they could mandate that telecoms ban
access by blacklisting exchanges and others in their infrastructure. China, in 2017 cracked
down on exchanges but not much happened, Bitcoin price only went higher in the weeks
following. Recently, I read of one company currently working on a global satellite network
that will broadcast blockchain data down to every corner of the planet so that people can use
Bitcoin without needing the internet.

The First Wave of Regulations

The New York State BitLicense was a part of the first wave of regulations to hit the crypto   Market. If your business involves New York or a New York State Resident, anyone engaging in any of the following is required to obtain a license:

- Virtual currency transmission

- Storing, holding, or maintaining custody or control of virtual currency on behalf of others

- Buying and selling virtual currency as a customer business

- Performing exchange services as a customer business

- Controlling, administering, or issuing a virtual currency

Undesirable Negatives

Untraceable digital currency, unfortunately does have a list of undesirable negatives. It can make
certain crimes easier to do, for example, kidnapping, extortion, tax evasion and the sale of illegal items. One example of this was the scandalous Silk Road website. It operated from February 2011 to October 2013. It was the largest online market for illegal drugs. Payments were made in Bitcoins, and the site held the coins for security while the goods were shipped.

Ross Ulbricht was the brain behind Silk Road. He went by several aliases, the best known were "Frosty" and "Dread Pirate Roberts." He tried to cover his trail, but the authorities were able to connect the dots. He was arrested in October 2013 and is now serving time in jail with a life sentence. The government seized 174,000 Bitcoins and they were later auctioned to the public.

The two lessons to be learned are, first, it's difficult to remain anonymous for a long time. The other, is that it's hard to move from the underground to the legitimate economy without attracting attention from law enforcement.

Chapter 6: Bitcoin and Altcoins Trading

Cryptos provide volatility, as traders we love this, it is sweet music for us. Why? If you place a trade and nothing happens then you have just paid the spread to your broker for nothing. Trading is a business (or you should treat it as one), for you to recover your cost of the transaction (the spread) you need and want volatility.

Rumors and panics add to the volatility. There can also be extreme sensitivity to news, 20% daily moves are **not** uncommon. The autumn of 2017, even by crypto standards, the volatility that we saw was astonishing.

Advantages

There are usually no trade size minimums, in contrast to trading stocks, commodities, or spot forex. You can also short sell, therefore an up or a down market are both okay with you. Other advantages are that you have the ability to trade directly with the exchanges, brokers are not mandatory. You can trade 24/7 which is even more trading hours than spot forex. Obviously, the liquidity is not equal throughout the day, some times of the day are more liquid than others.

Day Trading

Day trade with caution! For now you are trading mostly against inexperienced traders, but the scene is changing. The autumn of 2017 saw the launch of Europe's first Bitcoin mutual fund in France. There are also reports of several hedge and private funds with huge resources prepping to enter the market.

Market Timing

Getting in at the "perfect time" with Bitcoin and cryptocurrencies is unrealistic. What is going on, weekly double digits gains, is not supposed to, but it is. Using strictly technical analysis or fundamentals will fail you. Look to buy on panic drops, bounces upwards after Bitcoin panic drops have been very profitable. One tactic to deal with the volatility is to have price alerts set for noticeable price moves. I strongly suggest that you accumulate gradually, cryptocurrency wealth takes time. Ignore, as much as possible, the Wild West hype going on. If your crypto position has a 100% + move up, take some profits. If you did not have an existing position, after a major breakout upwards, buy on the pullbacks. The best opportunities are there for the informed and less emotional. This is especially true in an arena with crypto traders who are untested with facing 40-50% drops.

Leverage

Leverage? Use with caution and only with entities that offer reliable stop losses. Bitcoin and cryptos in general, are assets that can move 20-30% (either direction) on some days, therefore your account can easily blow up. You lose money when you get taken out, and that can easily happen with high leverage. Bottom line, stay in the game and any long-term shorting is with extreme caution...keep in mind all the "deaths" of Bitcoin.

Trading Alternate Currencies (Altcoins) & ICO's

- **Alternate Currencies (Altcoins)** The many alternative currencies that have sprung up based off of the idea and/or basic code of Bitcoin.

- **Initial Coin Offering (ICO)** is a way of crowdfunding via cryptocurrency. **ICO's** sell a right of <u>ownership or royalties</u>

<u>to a project</u>. A coin in an ICO is a symbol of ownership interest in an enterprise, a digital "certificate". Often confused with a **'token sale'** which refers to selling participation in an economy, giving investors <u>access to the features</u> of a project at a later date.

Before Trading or Investing, Keep in Mind

Many altcoins are useless, the early internet (.com) days all over again. Unfortunately, the scene is currently filled with swindlers and scammers eager to swindle those in the hunt for "overnight" riches. How to navigate the minefield? Search for the biggest gainers, go where the action is, BUT those gains need to backed up with trading volume. The altcoin volume needs to be 500,000 USD+ (for liquidity). The ICO needs a good value/selling proposition. What is the point of the coin? What problem does it solve? The backing team also needs to be top notch.

One of the more successful ICO's was Ethereum, they raised money with a token sale in 2014. In 2017 at least 90 Initial Coin Offerings have taken place raising 1 billion+ US Dollars. As of December 2017, there were also over 1,200 digital currencies.

Keep in mind with ICO's no one knows for sure which one will take off. If you invest in 5, there is a very good chance 3 to 4 will fail. But the one that does take off returns 10x or more. 10x means that if you invested $10mm, you generate $100mm in total when you sell.

A little tip: with ICO's or basic transactions, send fractions of payment to test transfers. Practice sending .001 for first few transactions, you can go out to 8 decimal places with Bitcoin.

You should be aware that many of the recent venture capital backed ventures have not brought their products to market as yet. In addition, the full uses of BTC and altcoins are just being explored. Many believe, with good reasons, that Bitcoin will be surpassed in value by another coin. Their basis is that rarely in technology does the first mover remain the dominant player after 5-10 years. Bottom line, we are in the early, early days of digital currencies.

SPOTTING THE ICO SCAMMERS!

Some of the best warning signs that you are dealing with scammers.

- Reaching them is difficult. The phone numbers they have can't be found by a simple web search
- The whitepaper is usually short (under 10 pages), filled with basic grammar or spelling errors
- The quality of the website is low or they used some free service to build it
- Their "about us" and registration details are questionable or missing
- The CEO or advisors can't be found on LinkedIn or other professional channels

Chapter 7: Trading Tactics

Here we will examine the major reasons why traders lose money and most important we will explore the solutions.

Unrealistic Expectations: It is important when getting into trading, as with many things, that one must have a realistic idea of what you are dealing with. Unrealistic expectations can take the form of someone starting with what is a mini-trader account of 1,000 or maybe 2,000 USD and expecting overnight riches.

You can even begin with 100 or 200 dollars, which is fine. There is nothing wrong with the amount, but those same traders at 100 or 200 dollars are expecting to have 1,000 or 2,000 dollars in their accounts within a couple days. There are firms out there that have actually mentioned or even promised them that they can do this. While I am not saying it is impossible, I am saying it is unrealistic. It is essential that you do have a sense of reality to your trading.

No Plan: Many people say "failing to plan is planning to fail", with planning, your trading is in alignment with your timeframe and the results that you are expecting to receive. A trading plan is essential, because without one you are setting yourself up for potentially huge losses. Without a plan there is no point in entering trading.

Too Much Risk: It could be the person with 100 dollars in their account or even 100,000. It is not the amount that is critical, but the amount you are risking in relation to the funds available. You begin from the position of making "failure survivable". This concept is based on the idea that your losses should not be catastrophic. For example, each position should not use more than 5 or 6% of your available risk capital. This will also mean that if leverage is used it should be a low amount.

Confusing Trading With Investing: In my years as a banker, I have had countless clients who I have had to repeatedly point out that they should not confuse the two. Trading is about making money short-term, it is income generating activity, you are moving in and out of trades. Investing is more long-term and usually has a minimum timeframe of a year. It could be that some of your investment goals are derived from your trading but do not confuse them. It may seem basic to some, but speaking from experience of advising clients globally there are still many out there that get trading and investment confused.

Solutions:

It's ok to talk about problems and challenges, but obviously we need to have some solutions.

Low Leverage: To avoid the problem of too much risk, a proven solution is using low leverage. You keep the leverage low because it gives you time to think, to react more effectively, and you are not as sensitive to changes in the market.

Scaling In Scaling Out: Scaling in scaling out is one of my favorites. I use it with investing and also with my trading. Scaling in scaling out, the theory behind it is that you allow the market to tell you which way to go, it is that simple. An example, I plan to buy 250 of GCMS altcoins after having done my technical and fundamental analysis. How to begin? I would start with a 25 or 50 coins position and allow the market to confirm if I am on the right path. If I bought GCMS coins at 100 dollars and they suddenly jump to 125 per coin, great, the market is confirming that I made the correct decision. In this example if I began with 25 coins, I would then add another 25 or 50 and repeat the process until I reach my goal of 250 coins.

There are some who might say I missed out a little on the move from 100 to 125 and I did somewhat, but I am also more secure in my decision by being patient. On the reverse, getting back to scaling out, let us imagine that the market had moved against me, instead of having 250 coins at risk initially, it would have been only 25. Obviously there is a trade off, but from experience, it is to the advantage of those who are scaling in scaling out.

Another example, let us say you bought 100 coins at 100 dollars each and the price suddenly drops to 90. What I would suggest, instead of selling everything immediately, that you consider selling only 25 or 30 because the drop could be due to an overreaction in the market. There are several things that could be at play, for example a false rumor, again you are allowing the market to guide you along the correct path. Of course if the price continues to fall then you decide on a final exit if it goes beyond your mental stop loss.

Trade Liquid Markets: To trade liquid markets is something I can't overemphasize. Having one, long shot type trade (with ultra-risk capital) is fine, as long as you are aware of the risk. However, for regular trading, the cryptos with low liquidity by cryptocurrency standards, are not my first choice. Liquidity is critical especially as a trader, an investor is not as time sensitive, but if you are trading where you might need to make sudden moves you want to be holding liquid cryptocurrencies.
Liquid, to be very clear, is the ability to move in and out of the trade with ease. Being in a trade and having paper profits is wonderful. However, when it is time to convert the paper profits into real ones and if you are unable to do so, then it is a bad joke as you can only watch them, not very nice. On the other side if you are in a loss and are unable to exit that position, it turns into a nightmare. I don't care who is giving tips, or whatever blog you are reading, you must trade liquid cryptocurrencies, there is no other way.

Selecting Cryptocurrencies: Select a few and get to know them well. As you can imagine no trader is trading 600 different coins at a time. A lot of people begin with cryptos by trading the most well-known ones, Bitcoin, Ethereum, for example. After a while, by trading a few selected cryptos they will become familiar to you and you will get a deeper sense of how they move.

Chapter 8: Putting It All Together

Traders must have a system. We will examine and connect the different aspects of a trading system.

Trading Platform: Selecting your trading platform is important because the platform is the vehicle that you use to conduct trading. Since the trading is online it is essential that you are using a platform that matches your style. It could be one that is either multi-asset or one that is more basic. You should know the provider behind the platform. With cryptocurrencies you have the option of using either a trading platform or dealing directly with an exchange. New exchanges are regularly popping up on the market and depending on the country you will need to be careful. I suggest that you get a recommendation from a friend or a trusted crypto advisor.

Goals: Without goals it is really difficult to begin trading. The analogy that I have heard and like to use, in regards to goals, is that without one it would be the equivalent of heading to a railway ticket counter and just say "give me a ticket!" and of course they would ask "a ticket to where?"
Short-term goals could be monthly or weekly profit targets, they are individualized. Goals must match your style and the amount of risk capital available for trading.

Long-term goals are often related to your investment strategy. They are also related to your short-term goals because the long-term goals should be based on the short-term profit targets. There must be a matchup, because if you have a weekly target of 100 dollars and a monthly target of a 1,000 then there is a discrepancy that needs to be addressed.

Mental Preparation: You do need to be psychologically ready to trade. If you are about to trade and are tense or nervous, then you need to take time off. Go meditate, get some exercise, do something else, but it is important that you do not trade until you are psychologically ready.

With trading you must have the mindset of not taking things personally. Remove emotions from trading, the goal is simply to make money.

Know your risk tolerance: How much are you willing to risk on each trade? It is important, remember traders' golden rule number one, "no cash, no trading." It doesn't matter what anyone tells you, if there is no cash, there is no trading and this must be taken seriously. This ties in with your risk tolerance, for example, having a cash balance of 10,000 USD and you want to risk 1%, the amount is 100 dollars. Meaning that of your risk capital, regardless of what you are trading, when you set your stop loss (mental or on a platform) it should not exceed 100 USD.

Do your due diligence: A new day has begun and your computer is on, what happened overnight? What happened on the crypto markets? You should be aware of the news that came out overnight and more importantly how the markets reacted to it. Sometimes, what in theory should be good news, the markets can surprise with a negative reaction.

How to select your entry level: Knowing your entry points means you have a good reason for every trade that you execute. If you do not have a good reason, I suggest that you take the funds and turn them over to a charity. When selecting your entry level, you need a good risk-reward ratio and this should match your risk tolerance. Technical/fundamental analysis is also taken into consideration. The support and resistance levels, news, are all essential before you execute any trade. If you are trading cryptos you need to be aware of where the support and resistance lines are for the time frame that you are trading.

Know Your Exit Levels: What is your profit target, is it a thousand dollars or a few? You need to be aware of this. When you are setting stops to control losses, the first thing to do is to ensure that they fall within your parameters. Same as with your entry level, you should know the fundamental analysis, support and resistance levels, and another traders' golden rule "cut your losses and let profits run." Many traders say the profits take care of themselves but you must keep a close eye on the losses.

Keep a Journal: It may not be for everyone but it is something that I use to record my trading. It includes several things, where I entered the trade, my exit level, and why I thought the trade was a good idea when I entered it. In review of your journal, if there are patterns, you will begin to detect them. You can either remove a pattern that is not working or expand on one that is. This helps you to fine-tune your trades.

Review Your Results: Review your profit or loss for the day. It is important because while trading can be fun, it is a business and the point is to make a profit. If in the review of your profit/loss you discover it is not what you had intended, your duty is to find out why. You also need to know what was behind your good results. Maybe it was pure luck, and if that was the case, great, but luck is normally not a sustainable strategy for trading. I would suggest, as I do in my trading, review your journal. Was it market news? Or was it the size of the positions? These factors can influence the results.

Transition From Demo to Live Trading

Tips on making a successful transition from a demo to a live _trading_ account (these are not _investing_ tips). These are several of the points that are discussed in the classes that I teach. First is realistic funding levels. Most demo accounts give you a huge amount of virtual money to trade with, but you don't have to use it all. In fact, it's better if you use the same amount of virtual money that you would actually fund your live account with. That way, you'll get a much better idea of how it will feel to lose or gain on those amounts, both mentally and physically. If you go from trading with hundreds of thousands of dollars in demo mode to trading with five or ten thousand in live mode, it will feel a lot different, and you will not have developed a money management strategy that works with those amounts. Therefore, if you have $5,000 to trade with, practice with $5,000 in your demo account.

Next is reality-based expected trading sizes. As with the funding levels, you need to make trades of the similar size in demo mode as you might reasonably expect to do in live mode. This ensures parity with the strategy that you will be using in live mode. You will have a much smoother transition. If you are planning to trade small sizes with your funded account, trade small in demo mode so that you know what you are getting into in terms of leverage(if you use it).

Profitable trading: If you're making a loss every week in demo trading, then it's unwise to make the switch to live trading, as it's your real money that you'll be losing. While you can't expect to make a profit every day, you should be coming out ahead at the end of every month before you even consider a switch to a live funded trading account.

Chapter 9: Crypto Technical Analysis Toolbox

The key point to making money with technical analysis is identifying the trend and trading along with it. Trends reveal to you where prices are most likely to head in the future. If the trend of a crypto is heading up, then you need to buy the crypto to make money. If the trend of a crypto is beginning to go lower, you need to sell the crypto to profit. If the trend of a crypto is sideways, with no clear direction, you either need to place contingent orders (not trades) or wait until a clear trend up or down is established before trading. It is not recommended to fight the trend, if you elect to do so, in most cases it will be an expensive experience for **you**.

Trends do not normally move straight up or straight down in a direct fashion. They usually move in one direction for a period of time and then temporarily retrace (reverse) part of the previous movement before continuing back on the original direction. Every time a crypto retraces and begins moving in the opposite direction, it forms a new high or a new low. For example, with cryptos, new highs form when a crypto moves higher and then turns around and moves lower. New lows form when a crypto moves lower and then turns around and moves higher. Identifying these highs and lows allows you to identify whether a crypto is in an uptrend, a downtrend or a sideways trend.

Uptrends - Markets that are trending upward form a series of higher highs and higher lows.

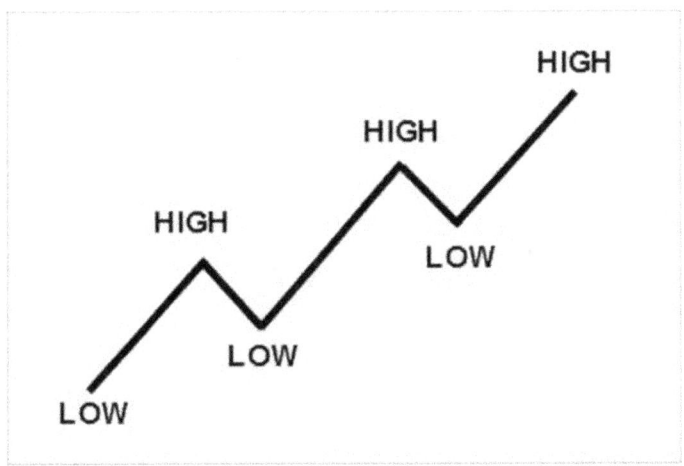

Downtrends - Markets that are trending downward form a series of lower highs and lower lows.

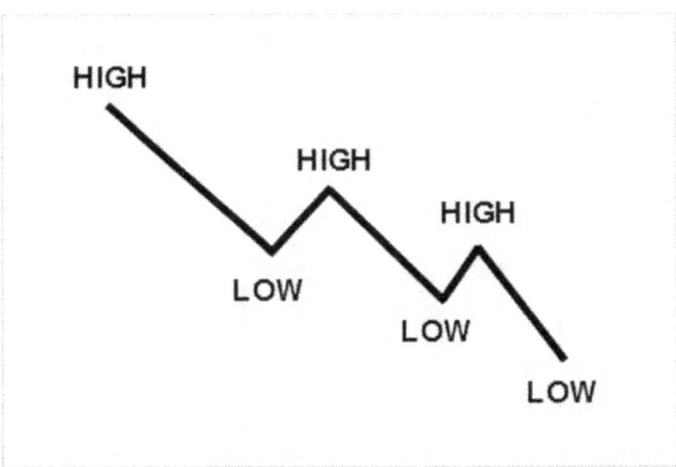

Sideways trends - A cryptocurrency that is trending sideways form a series of highs that are at approximately the same price level and a series of lows that are at approximately the same price level.

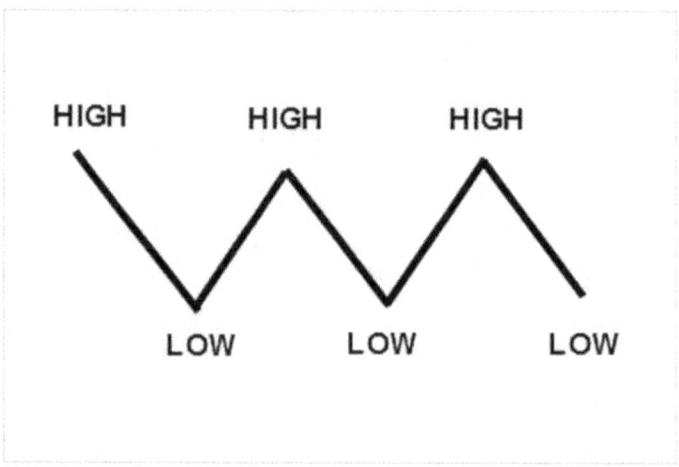

Trends - Whether they are uptrends, downtrends or sideways, trends can form over various time periods. Identifying the different trends over each timeframe and being able to align them in your analysis is crucial to your success as a trader.

Defining a candlestick chart

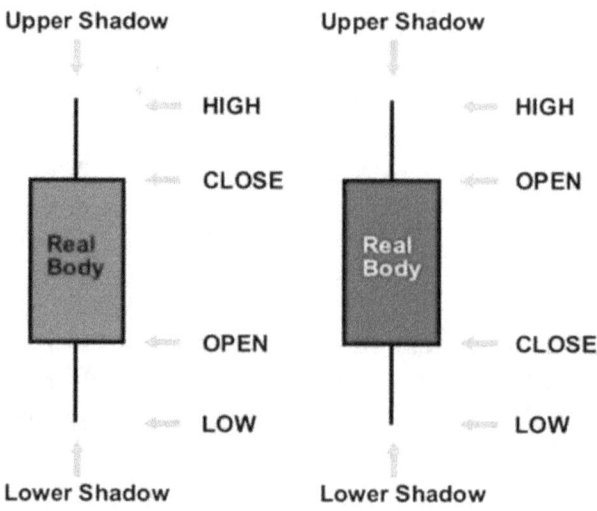

Let us begin by defining a candlestick. A candlestick is a line on a chart which represents one point and shows the high, low, open and close for each period. For example, if we have a daily chart, each candlestick represents one day and will show the high, low, open and close for that day. On many platforms, a red candlestick means that the close price is lower than the open price for that period. A green candlestick means that the close price is higher than the open price for that period.

Technical Analysis Indicators

We will take a look at the Moving Averages, RSI and Bollinger Bands indicators. First is the Moving Averages, and they are useful because they make it easier to spot a trend. This is key with currencies, cryptocurrencies or some of the derivatives where an up market is good and a down market is also good. Therefore, all we need to do is to identify or spot this trend. To illustrate, a fifty-day moving average adds up the closing prices for the last fifty days, divide by fifty and plots a point on the chart for each day.

Moving Average Chart

Let us review some basic settings with the moving average indicator. If we have settings on a chart of MA ten, MA fifty, then ten is the short-term, fifty is the long-term. The shorter moving average, if that is above the longer, the trend is considered upward. If the shorter moving average is below the longer moving average, then the trends is considered downward. On a chart if you see that the ten is breaking beneath the fifty, the long-term in this example, that could be taken as the initial sign of a sell signal.

With moving averages the buy and sell signals are generated by the price crossing above or below the moving average line. There is a term that you will hear a lot if you are around technical analysis folks, it is called the *golden cross* and it means that the short-term breaks above the long- term. The example we have is ten and fifty, but it could have been twenty and thirty, fifteen and seventeen, it depends on the trader and the instrument that they are trading.

Relative Strength Index

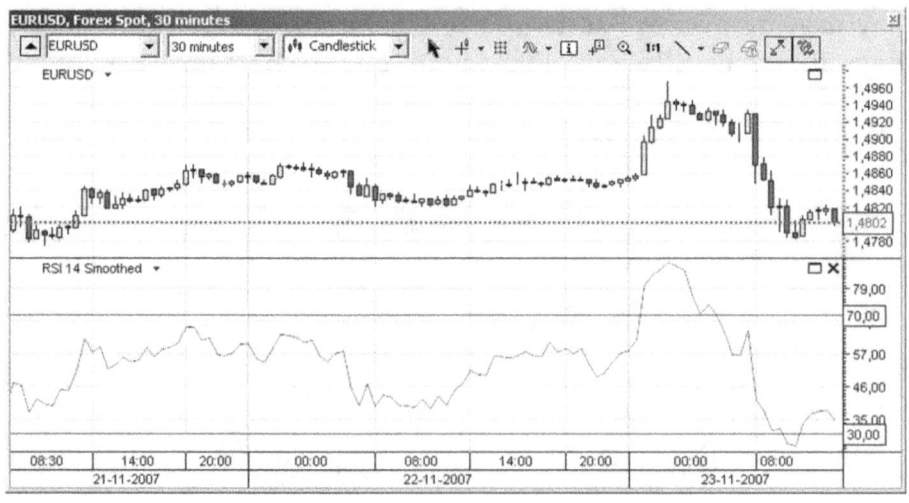

The RSI, which is the Relative Strength Index is used to identify if the market (stock, currency, cryptocurrency, etc.) is overbought or oversold. It is classified as a leading indicator because it begins giving signals before the trend has begun. It has an index from zero to one hundred.

The RSI graph is visible beneath the EURUSD chart. The RSI matches more or less what is happening on the chart and it should. Readings below thirty indicate that the market maybe oversold and when you see or hear the term oversold it mean excessive selling. Readings above seventy indicate that the market maybe overbought, excessive buying. Keep in mind these are indications, they are not guarantees of anything. As a note, the market can remain overbought or oversold for a considerable period of time.

Bollinger Bands

Bollinger Bands are a tool that many investors and traders use when they want to add different technical analysis aspects to the trades that they have open. They are used to measure market volatility. The bands define the upper and lower limits of the trading range. When you view the bands on a chart, you will have a top and a bottom band. The space between the top and the bottom, is called the buy - sell channel. You use the space between the bands to get an idea of where you are within the trading range. If you are near the top, you know that you are close to the resistance level and there is a potential for a price reversal (the market reverses direction). If you are at the bottom, you know that you are near the support level for a potential price reversal there. For the most part prices do remain between the bands. If the price begins to break out, many traders take this as a signal so you do need to be aware of that.

Understanding Support and Resistance Levels

Support level is the price level at which the instrument traded has historically had difficulty falling below. For example, if we have support around 1.4380, you would be able to see on a chart that the market has been to that level (1.4380) several times without falling lower, so in technical analysis jargon this would be considered a support level. Resistance level is just the opposite, the price level at which the instrument has historically had difficulty trading above.

Chart patterns similar to the letters M & W

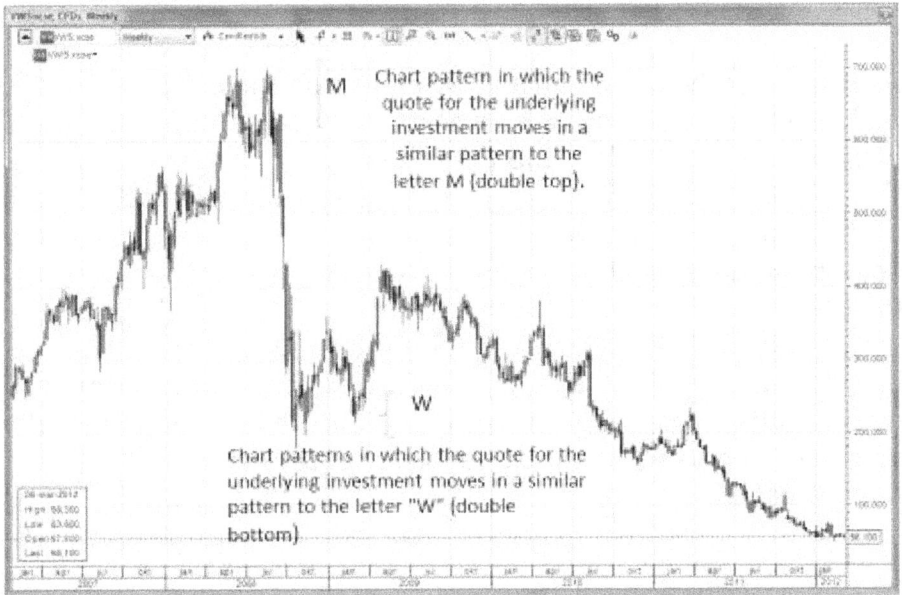

M Chart pattern in which the quote for the underlying investment moves in a similar pattern to the letter M (double top).

W

Chart patterns in which the quote for the underlying investment moves in a similar pattern to the letter "W" (double bottom).

Chart Patterns "W" Double Bottom or "M" Double Top

These are chart patterns in which the price quoted for the instrument moves in a pattern similar to the letter "W" (double bottom) or "M" (double top). Double top and bottom patterns are used in technical analysis to explain movements in a stock, cryptocurrency or other investments, and can be used as part of a trading strategy to exploit recurring patterns. A double top and a double bottom are both trend reversal patterns.

A **double bottom** tends to occur after a strong downtrend, and it indicates that an uptrend may be imminent. The "bottoms" are valleys which are formed when the price hits a certain support level that cannot be broken. After hitting this level, the price will bounce off it slightly before returning to test the level again. If the price bounces off the support a second time, then you have a double bottom formation. If the second bottom cannot break the low of the first, then this is a strong signal that a reversal is going to happen. A ´neckline´ is drawn at the high between the two ´bottoms´. With a double bottom, you could think of placing your long (buy) entry order above the 'neckline' because you are expecting the trend to change upwards.

A **double top** is usually formed after an extended uptrend, and it indicates that a downtrend may be imminent. The "tops" are peaks which are formed when the price hits a certain resistance level that cannot be broken. After hitting this level, the price will bounce off it slightly, but then return back to test the level again. If the price bounces off of that level again, then you have a double top. If the second top cannot break the high of the first top, then this is a strong signal that a reversal is going to happen. A 'neckline' is drawn at the low between the two 'tops'. With a double top, you could think of placing your short (sell) entry order below the 'neckline' because you are expecting the trend to change downwards.

Chapter 10: The Most Common Arguments Against Bitcoin and Cryptos - With Answers

Credit cards and cash are accepted by most merchants, but Bitcoin has little acceptance:

Currently this is mostly true but the reality is changing. There are now more than 150,000 merchants globally that accept Bitcoin as a payment method. In early 2014 overstock.com became the first major retailer to accept Bitcoin. Other firms that accept payments include, Subway, Wordpress, Virgin Galactic, Reddit, Wikipedia, Shopify, OKCupid, Amazon, Paypal, and Ebay. There is more, in late November 2017 one of the Big Four accounting firms, PricewaterhouseCoopers, said it accepted a payment in Bitcoin for its advisory services.

A key point to keep in mind is that cryptocurrencies are not fiat currencies. They only become similar to a fiat when a government says they are legal tender. If that were to happen, then yes, your local bike or coffee shop would have to accept them whenever you choose to spend them.

Government powers are not giving up their control of money without a fight. They will crush cryptocurrencies:

The possibility and risk of government intervention exists, but there is no growing movement to do this. A few countries have banned them and their prices and acceptance by the general public has only grown. Even among the banners, only certain activities have been banned, for example ICO's.

Bitcoin and other cryptos are benefiting from first mover advantages but what about future competition?

No need to wait for the future, competitors already exist. So far the market value of the top first mover cryptos has only increased. The most popular cryptos are mainly used to store or grow wealth. In other words, many people are buying cryptos simply because they expect the price to increase. The competition provides people more options, but it has not destroyed any of the top players. For example, just because a new company is listed on the stock exchange that doesn't automatically mean their competitors will collapse. Many investors simply prefer to diversify.

Chapter 11: What to Expect in The Near Future

I purposely used what to expect in the near future, because making any long-term claims about cryptos is a fool's errand in my view.

Less ICO Madness

The ICO madness will lose some of the irrational gold rush mentality and we will see improved self-policing from the current players in the market. The public and government regulators do have limits on what they will tolerate.

Relevant Regulations

Trading in Bitcoin and other cryptocurrencies remains mostly unregulated. I was recently made aware of the amount of agencies that claim jurisdiction over cryptocurrencies. This is just in the United States alone, you have the Treasury Department's FinCEN, the Securities and Exchange Commission, and the Internal Revenue Service (IRS). The story gets more bizarre, because there isn't even agreement among the regulators on what a Bitcoin is. For example, the IRS treats it as property and the Commodity Futures Trading Commission says it is a commodity. For market participants this bring confusion to new levels. Even with the confusion, to increase the trust of the broader retail and institutional markets, there is a need of more appropriate regulations for this growing market. This should also include swift and robust punishment for those engaging in misconduct.

Waiting to see more of

What I am eagerly awaiting to see more of in the near crypto future.

1-Exchanges will upgrade both security and their capacity to deal with demand surges. Even though crypto exchanges are not subjected to the same level of scrutiny as traditional exchanges, going forward this security issue will become increasingly difficult to keep talking around. Why? the crypto landscape has enough sad tales of hackings with millions being stolen. No region in the world gets to point fingers. It happens in the East and it also happens in the West, to both big and small exchanges. In contrast to funds in your local bank, if your account is hacked at an exchange, there is very little recourse to recovering your funds and as of this writing there is no insurance available. Everyone knows hackers are on a dedicated hunt after cryptocurrency accounts, therefore the defense needs to step up. The internal threats are another set of headaches, they range from insider trading to other financial misconduct from employees.

Several of the regulated and larger exchanges buckled under demand for new accounts during the recent market explosions. They will get a pass this time around, but how many more times will the public or those in power remain so forgiving?

2- Autumn 2017 saw the launch of Bitcoin futures and it will be interesting to see how this plays out. The public has been asking for a more regulated market, well trading on a futures exchange is all about regulations. This is also the first time that Bitcoin traders can hedge their position in a regulated market. They can now take the other side in the market, by shorting.

3- More coins that eliminates the need for miners. Currently, the majority of Bitcoin mining is done by a handful of firms. Not a market healthy situation as they can use this influence in undesirable ways.

4-Improvements in the speed of transactions seems to be catching the attention of many industry influencers. Even for Bitcoin fans, the relatively slow pace of a routine transaction can be an issue. There are several cryptos that are taking on these challenges and I'm excited to see how their stories develop.

Bitcoin and cryptocurrencies have travelled far from the days of when they were mostly associated with criminals. Now there is both a broader and more positive public awareness. Bitcoin futures transactions are even cleared by top name Wall Street firms, something, that not along ago would have been laughed at. For progress to continue as I have laid out, there needs to be less hype, relevant regulations, and greater security plus transparency from the exchanges. These suggestions I believe will secure that cryptocurrencies, as an asset class, moves beyond the early adopters phase.

Conclusion

Thank you for making it through to the end of *The Definitive Guide to Mastering Bitcoin & Cryptocurrencies.* Let's hope it was informative and able to provide you with the tools that you need to achieve your goals of trading cryptocurrencies and making money. The next step is to test your skills at trading and build up your risk capital. This will give you the motivation that you need to succeed. I have several other books on different aspects of trading and asset classes please check them out!

PROFILE OF THE AUTHOR

Wayne Walker is the founder of GCMS, a leading capital markets education and consulting firm (gcmsonline.info). He is an authority on cryptocurrency trading and education. In addition to launching the first cryptocurrency training course in Northern Europe, he is also a well-read author and guest journalist at Cryptcoin.news one of the leading voices in the industry. Those serious about trading and investing in cryptocurrencies are encouraged to contact GCMS.

Essential Bitcoin Vocabulary

Blockchain: Is a **public** record/ledger of Bitcoin transactions in chronological order. The blockchain is shared amongst all Bitcoin users. It is used to verify the permanence of Bitcoin transactions and to prevent double spending.

Block: Is <u>a record in the blockchain</u> that contains and confirms waiting transactions. Roughly every 10 minutes, on average, a new block including transactions is created to the blockchain through mining.

Genesis Block: This is the very first block that was created and the beginning of the blockchain.

Hash Rate: Is the measuring unit of the processing power of the Bitcoin network. The Bitcoin network must make intensive mathematical operations for security purposes. When the network reached a hash rate of 10 Th/s, it meant it could make 10 trillion calculations per second.

Mining: Is the process of making computer hardware do mathematical calculations for the Bitcoin network to confirm transactions and increase security. As a reward for their services, Bitcoin miners can collect transaction fees for the transactions they confirm, along with newly created bitcoins. Mining is specialized and competitive the rewards are divided up according to how much calculation is done.

Confirmation: Confirmation means that a transaction has been processed by the network and is highly unlikely to be reversed. Transactions receive a confirmation when they are included in a block and for each subsequent block. Even a single confirmation can be considered secure for low value transactions, although for larger amounts like 1000 US$, it makes sense to wait for several more confirmations.

Double Spend: If a malicious user tries to spend their bitcoins to two different recipients at the same time, this is double spending. Bitcoin mining and the block chain are there to create a consensus on the network about which of the two transactions will confirm and be considered valid.

Private Key: Is a secret piece of data that proves your right to spend bitcoins from a specific wallet through a cryptographic signature. Your private key(s) are stored in your computer if you use a software wallet; they are stored on some remote servers if you use a web wallet. Private keys must never be revealed as they allow you to spend bitcoins for their respective Bitcoin wallet.

Signature: A cryptographic signature is a mathematical mechanism that allows someone to prove ownership. In the case of Bitcoin, a Bitcoin wallet and its private key(s) are linked by mathematical magic. When your Bitcoin software signs a transaction with the appropriate private key, the whole network can see that the signature matches the bitcoins being spent. However, there is no way for the world to guess your private key to steal your bitcoins.

Wallet: A Bitcoin wallet is loosely the equivalent of a physical wallet on the Bitcoin network. The wallet actually contains your private key(s) which allow you to spend the bitcoins allocated to it in the blockchain. Each Bitcoin wallet can show you the total balance of all bitcoins it controls and lets you pay an amount to a specific person.

Cold Storage: This is the process of moving your bitcoins to an offline wallet. The benefit of this is that no one can hack into your computer and steal your private keys if your computer is not connected to a network. Bitcoins will need to be brought back out of cold storage to be spent or transferred again.

Address: A Bitcoin address is a unique string of 27-34 alphanumeric characters. An address can be created freely with the use of a wallet and always starts with a 1 or a 3.

Alternate Currencies: The many different alternative currencies that have sprung up based off of the idea and/or basic code of Bitcoin. A few of the more notable ones are Litecoin, IOTA, and Ripple.

Fork: A "fork" is a change to the software of the digital currency that creates two separate versions of the blockchain with a shared history. Forks can be temporary or they can be a permanent split in the network creating two separate versions of the blockchain. When this happens, two different digital currencies are also created.

DDOS: Short for 'Distributed Denial of Service'. A well-timed DDoS attack at exchanges during volatile movements may be devastating as traders will not be able to execute any order manually and will be at the mercy of their pre-set orders.

*Infographic from Chapter 2 was created by CB Insights.